JONNY ZUCKER began his career in radio
and is now a writer and primary school teacher. Along the way
he has played in several bands and has worked as
a stand-up comedian. Jonny has written two books for adults:
A Class Act and *Dream Decoder*. He lives in London
with his wife and their young son.

JAN BARGER'S previous titles include
Bible Stories for the Very Young, *Busy Town*, the Little Animals series,
Incy Wincy Moo-Cow, *Who Can Fly?*, *Who Eats This?*
and *Who Lives Here?*

80 002 595 039

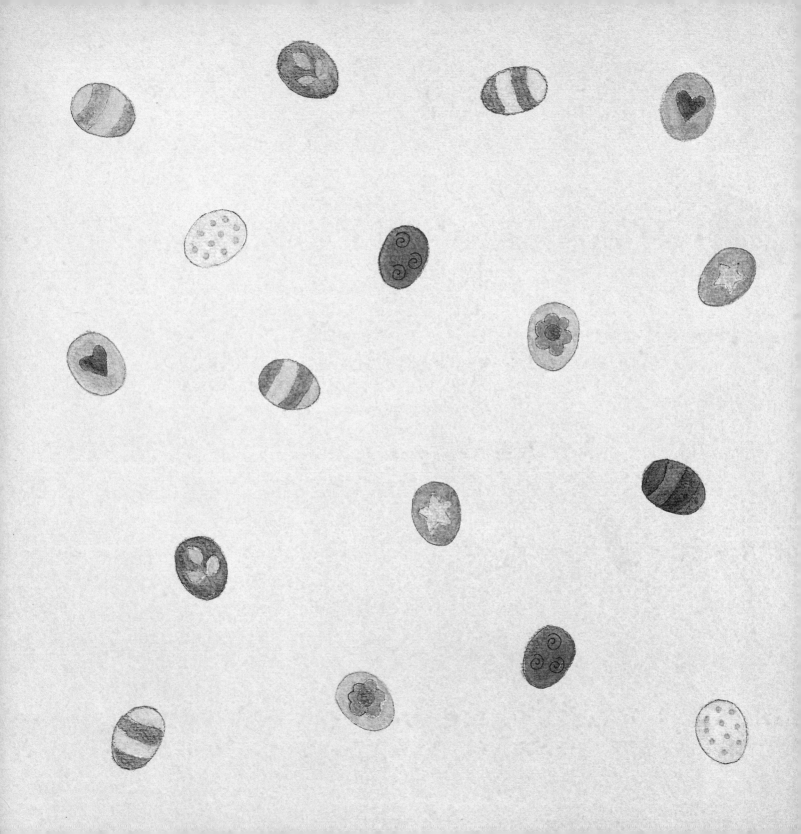

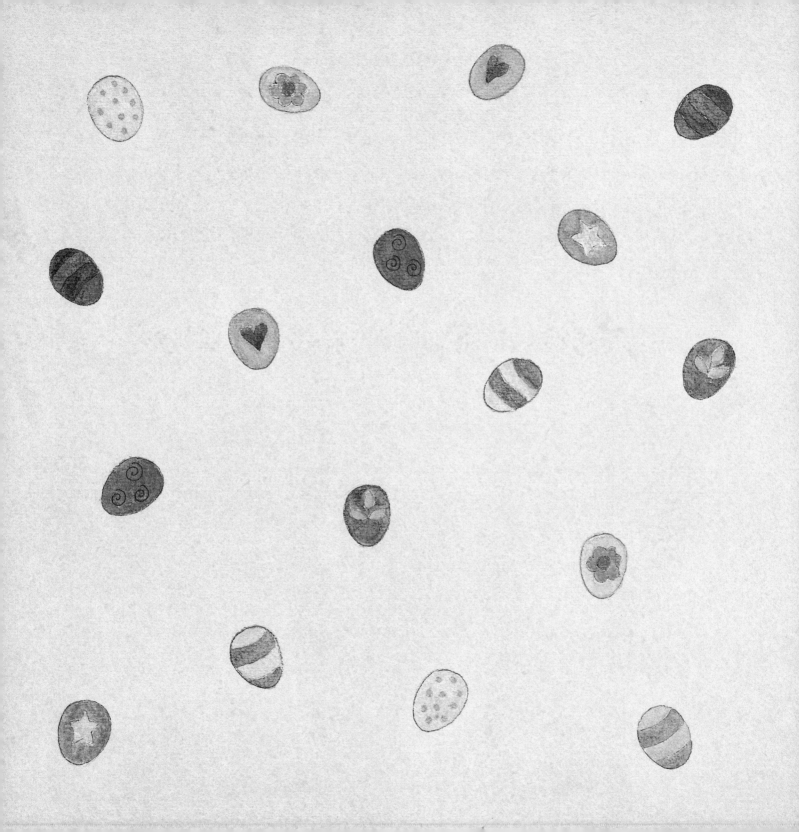

For Wendy and John – J.Z.
For Judy – J.B.

FESTIVAL TIME!

Hope and New Life!

An Easter Story

Jonny Zucker

Illustrated by Jan Barger

FRANCES LINCOLN CHILDREN'S BOOKS

It's Palm Sunday –
the beginning of Holy Week.
We remember how Jesus rode
into Jerusalem on a donkey.

On Maundy Thursday, Mum, Dad
and my older sister eat bread
and drink wine to remind us of
Jesus's Last Supper with his disciples.

On Good Friday we go to church
and hear how Jesus died
on the cross to save us.

We paint eggs
and eat sticky
hot cross buns.

It's Easter Sunday,
and we go to church
and sing songs to celebrate
how Jesus came back to life.

I'm going on an Easter egg hunt.
The Easter bunny has hidden
chocolate eggs in the garden
and I find some!

On Easter Monday we watch a parade
and feel happy to be celebrating
our festival of hope and new life.

What is Easter About?

Long ago, Jesus lived in Israel in the region of Lake Galilee. He healed many people and taught them about God and how to live good lives.

One Sunday, he rode into Jerusalem on a donkey and all his friends walked in behind. Crowds of people came out to cheer and they cut down palm branches and waved them in celebration. We remember this happening on **Palm Sunday**, the Sunday before Easter Day, and churchgoers receive a palm cross to remind them.

Four days later, on Thursday, Jesus invited his twelve friends to supper in a room upstairs in a house in Jerusalem. This is known as the **Last Supper**, because it was the last meal he ate with his friends. At supper, he broke a loaf of bread and said to his friends, "this is my body", and took a cup of wine and said, "this is my blood". Jesus knew he was about to die and he said this so that his friends would have a way of remembering his death.

Every week in church, Christians eat bread and drink wine to remember Jesus's death. This is called the **Holy Communion** or **Mass**.

After supper, Jesus went to pray in a garden with his friends, and while he was there, soldiers came to arrest him because Jesus's teachings frightened the Romans who were in charge. They put Jesus on trial before the Governor of Israel who was called Pontius Pilate.

It was decided that Jesus should die on a cross. We remember this on **Good Friday**. It is called Good Friday because Christians believe that when Jesus died he took away all the sin, or bad things that we do, and as a result of his death, God forgave us. When we eat hot cross buns, we see the cross on the bun to remind us of Jesus's death.

When Jesus died, nearly all his friends were afraid and ran away, but a woman called Mary Magdalene saw where they put Jesus's body in a tomb after he died. On Sunday, she went to the tomb to look after Jesus's body. Imagine her surprise to find that the tomb was empty. She saw an angel, who told her that Jesus had come back to life again. Later, she saw Jesus for herself.

Every year, we remember on **Easter Sunday** that Jesus died and rose again from the dead to live forever in heaven. Easter eggs are eaten, because eggs are a sign of new life, and Christians are happy at this time of year. Because Jesus came back to life, we know that we, too, can live forever with him in heaven.

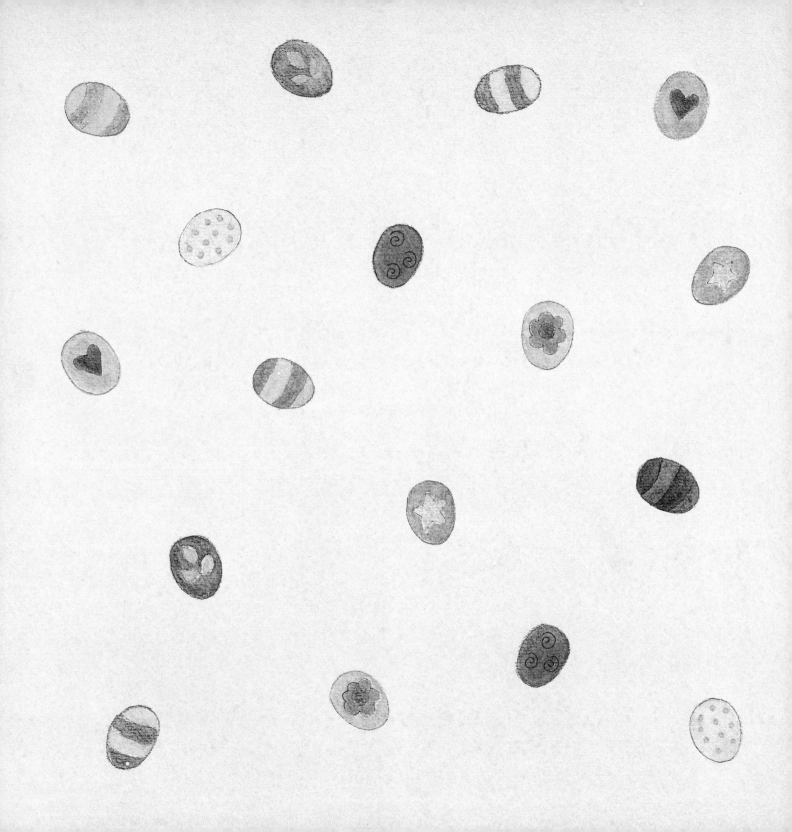

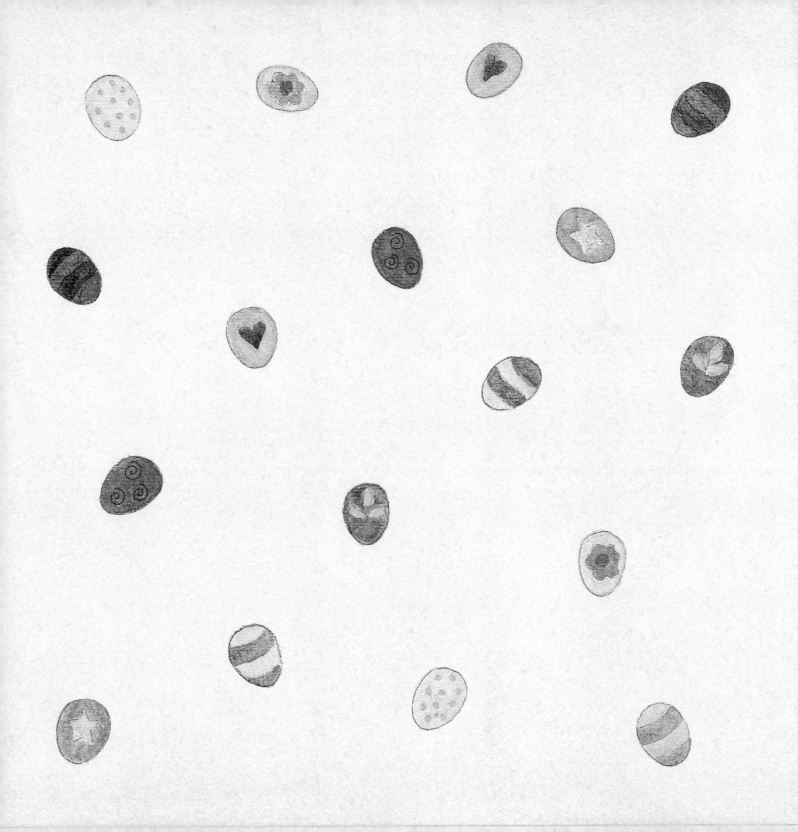

MORE TITLES IN THE FESTIVAL TIME! SERIES BY JONNY ZUCKER

Lanterns and Firecrackers – A Chinese New Year Story

Follow a family as they let off firecrackers,
watch lion and dragon dances and hang up lanterns
to celebrate the start of their New Year.

ISBN 1-84507-000-3

Sweet Dates to Eat – A Ramadan and Eid Story

Follow a family as they fast each day,
go to the mosque on the Night of Power,
and enjoy a delicious feast.

ISBN 1-84507-063-1

Lighting a Lamp – A Divali Story

Follow a family as they make rangoli patterns, light divas
and watch a brilliant firework display to celebrate
their amazing festival of light.

ISBN 1-84507-062-3

Frances Lincoln titles are available from all good bookshops.
You can also buy books and find out more about your favourite titles,
authors and illustrators on our website: www.franceslincoln.com